# 100 POP SOLOS
## FOR CLARINET

100 POP SOLOS

100 POP SOLOS

100 POP SOLOS

EXCLUSIVE DISTRIBUTORS:

MUSIC SALES LIMITED, 8/9 FRITH STREET, LONDON W1V 5TZ, ENGLAND.

MUSIC SALES PTY LIMITED, 120 ROTHSCHILD AVENUE, ROSEBERY, NSW 2018, AUSTRALIA.

ORDER NO. AM958716

ISBN 0-7119-8203-1

THIS BOOK © COPYRIGHT 2000 BY WISE PUBLICATIONS.

COMPILED BY NICK CRISPIN.

MUSIC ARRANGED BY JACK LONG.

MUSIC PROCESSED BY ENIGMA MUSIC PRODUCTION SERVICES.

COVER DESIGN BY PHIL GAMBRILL.

COVER PHOTOGRAPHS COURTESY OF LONDON FEATURES INTERNATIONAL.

PRINTED AND BOUND IN MALTA.

YOUR GUARANTEE OF QUALITY:

AS PUBLISHERS, WE STRIVE TO PRODUCE EVERY BOOK TO THE HIGHEST COMMERCIAL STANDARDS.

THE MUSIC HAS BEEN FRESHLY ENGRAVED AND THE BOOK HAS BEEN CAREFULLY

DESIGNED TO MINIMISE AWKWARD PAGE TURNS AND TO MAKE PLAYING FROM IT A REAL PLEASURE.

PARTICULAR CARE HAS BEEN GIVEN TO SPECIFYING ACID-FREE, NEUTRAL-SIZED PAPER MADE

FROM PULPS WHICH HAVE NOT BEEN ELEMENTAL CHLORINE BLEACHED.

THIS PULP IS FROM FARMED SUSTAINABLE FORESTS AND WAS PRODUCED WITH SPECIAL REGARD FOR THE ENVIRONMENT.

THROUGHOUT, THE PRINTING AND BINDING HAVE BEEN PLANNED TO ENSURE A STURDY,

ATTRACTIVE PUBLICATION WHICH SHOULD GIVE YEARS OF ENJOYMENT.

IF YOUR COPY FAILS TO MEET OUR HIGH STANDARDS, PLEASE INFORM US AND WE WILL GLADLY REPLACE IT.

MUSIC SALES' COMPLETE CATALOGUE DESCRIBES THOUSANDS OF TITLES AND

IS AVAILABLE IN FULL COLOUR SECTIONS BY SUBJECT, DIRECT FROM MUSIC SALES LIMITED.

PLEASE STATE YOUR AREAS OF INTEREST AND SEND A CHEQUE/POSTAL ORDER FOR £1.50 FOR POSTAGE TO:

MUSIC SALES LIMITED, NEWMARKET ROAD, BURY ST. EDMUNDS, SUFFOLK IP33 3YB.

www.musicsales.com

100 POP SOLOS

**WISE PUBLICATIONS**

LONDON / NEW YORK / PARIS / SYDNEY / COPENHAGEN / MADRID / TOKYO

# All That I Need

Words & Music by Evan Rogers & Carl Sturken

# All That She Wants

Words & Music by Jonas Berggren & Ulf Ekberg

# American Pie

Words & Music by Don McLean

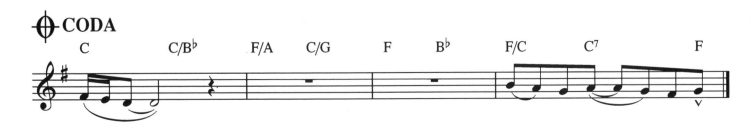

# Angels

Words & Music by Robbie Williams & Guy Chambers

# As Long As You Love Me

Words & Music by Max Martin

# Baby One More Time

Words & Music by Max Martin

# Barbie Girl

Words & Music by Søren Rasted, Claus Norreen, Rene Dif,
Lene Nystrom, Johnny Pederson & Karsten Delgado

11

# Big Mistake

Words & Music by Natalie Imbruglia & Mark Goldenberg

# Blame It On The Weatherman

Words & Music by Ray Hedges, Martin Brannigan, Andy Caine & Tracy Ackerman

# Blinded By The Sun

Words & Music by Chris Helme

# Bootie Call

Words & Music by Shaznay Lewis & Karl Gordon

# Bring It All Back

Words & Music by Eliot Kennedy, Mike Percy, Tim Lever & S Club 7

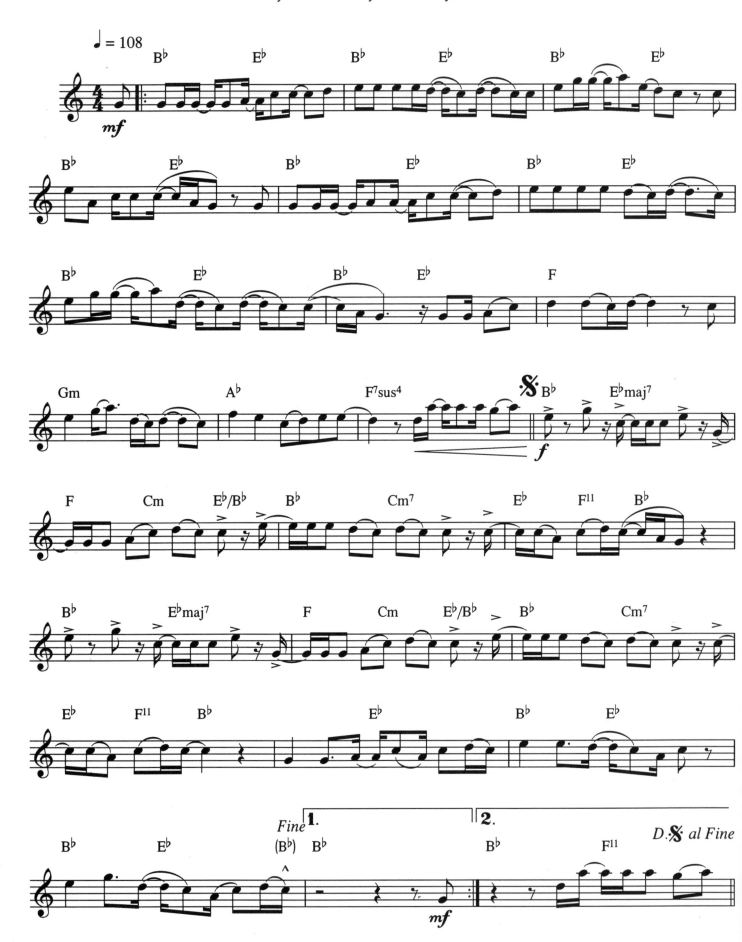

# Brothers In Arms

Words & Music by Mark Knopfler

# C'est La Vie

Words & Music by Edele Lynch, Keavy Lynch, Lindsay Armaou,
Sinead O'Carroll, Ray Hedges, Martin Brannigan & Tracey Ackerman

# Call The Man

Words & Music by Andy Hill & Peter Sinfield

# Can't Help Falling In Love

Words & Music by George Weiss, Hugo Peretti & Luigi Creatore

# Candle In The Wind

Words & Music by Elton John & Bernie Taupin

# Could It Be Magic

Words & Music by Barry Manilow & Adrienne Anderson

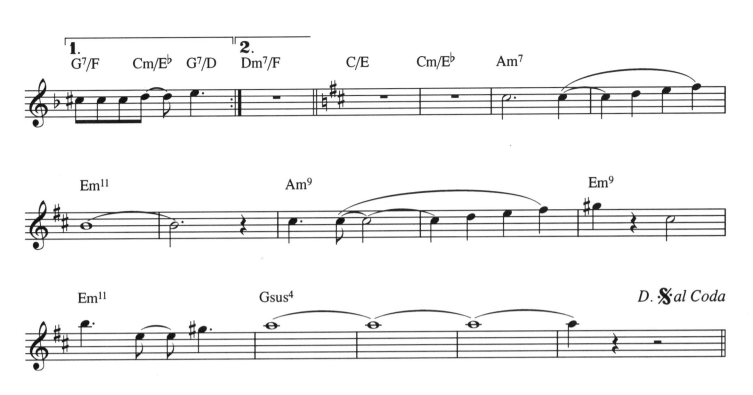

# Crying

Words & Music by Roy Orbison & Joe Melson

# Dead From The Waist Down

Words & Music by Cerys Matthews, Mark Roberts, Aled Richards, Paul Jones & Owen Powell

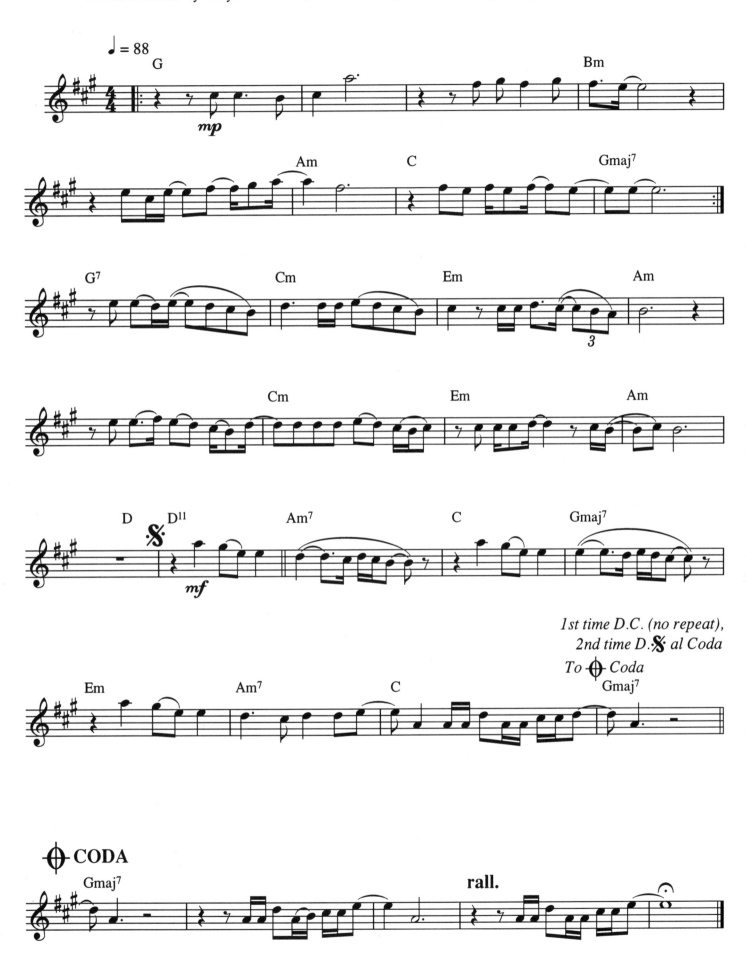

1st time D.C. (no repeat),
2nd time D.S. al Coda

To ⊕ Coda

# Diva

Words by Yoav Ginai
Music by Svika Pick

# Don't Look Back In Anger

Words & Music by Noel Gallagher

# Don't You Love Me

Words & Music by Cynthia Biggs, Carolyn Mitchell, Terence Dudley & Christopher Kellum

# Englishman In New York

Words & Music by Sting

# Falling Into You

Words & Music by Rick Nowels, Marie-Claire D'Ubaldo & Billy Steinberg

# Female Of The Species

Words & Music by Tommy Scott, James Edwards, Francis Griffiths & Andrew Parle

# Good Enough

Words & Music by Nigel Clark, Mathew Priest & Andy Miller

# Have I Told You Lately

Words & Music by Van Morrison

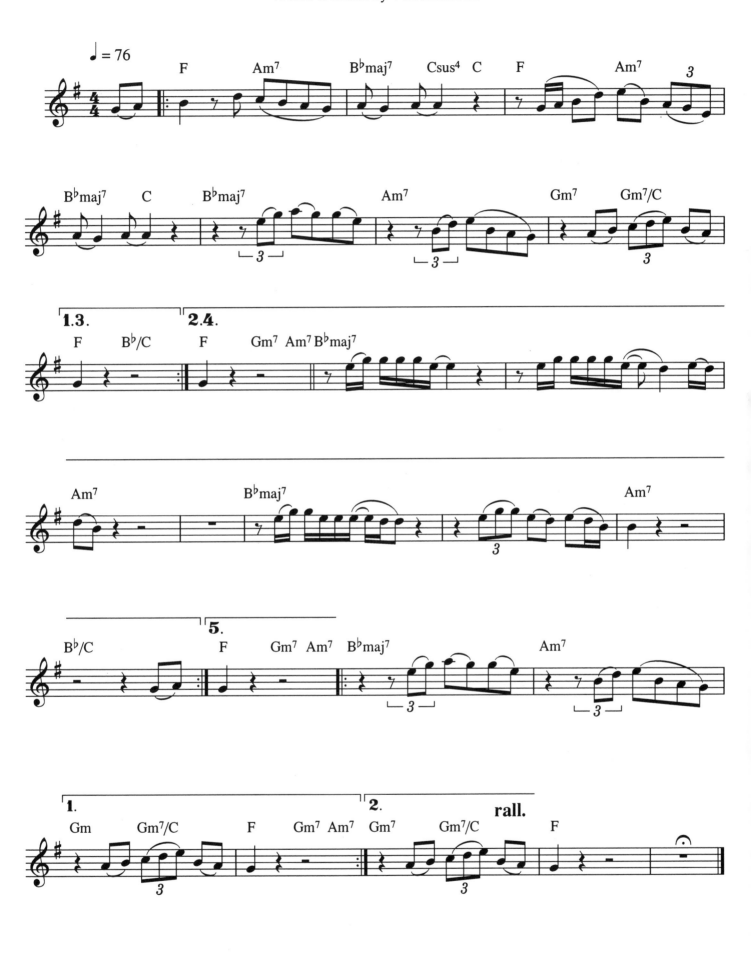

# Help The Aged

Words by Jarvis Cocker

Music by Jarvis Cocker, Nick Banks, Candida Doyle, Steve Mackey & Mark Webber

# High

Words by Paul Tucker
Music by Paul Tucker & Tunde Baiyewu

# I Believe I Can Fly

Words & Music by R. Kelly

# I Have A Dream

Words & Music by Benny Andersson & Björn Ulvaeus

# I Love The Way You Love Me

Words & Music by Chuck Cannon & Victoria Shaw

# I Say A Little Prayer

Words by Hal David
Music by Burt Bacharach

# I Will Always Love You

Words & Music by Dolly Parton

# If You Ever

Words & Music by Carl Martin

# In The Air Tonight

Words & Music by Phil Collins

# Knockin' On Heaven's Door

Words & Music by Bob Dylan

# Killing Me Softly With His Song

Words by Norman Gimbel
Music by Charles Fox

# La Copa De La Vida (The Cup Of Life)

Words & Music by Robi Rosa, Desmond Child & Luis Gomez Escolar

# Last Thing On My Mind

Words by Sarah Dallin & Keren Woodward
Music by Mike Stock & Pete Waterman

# Let It Be

Words & Music by John Lennon & Paul McCartney

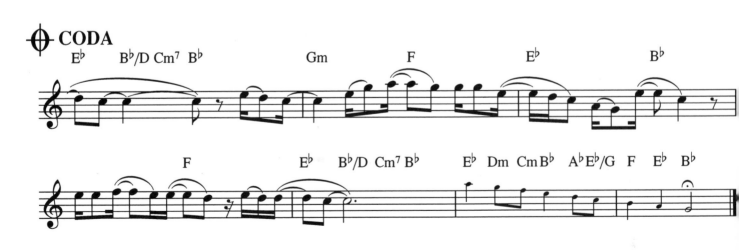

# Let Me Entertain You

Words & Music by Robbie Williams & Guy Chambers

# Like A Virgin

Words & Music by Billy Steinberg & Tom Kelly

# Livin' La Vida Loca

### Words & Music by Desmond Child & Robi Rosa

# Livin' On A Prayer

Words & Music by Jon Bon Jovi, Richie Sambora & Desmond Child

# Lost In Space

Words by Paul Tucker
Music by Paul Tucker & Tim Laws

# Love Is All Around

Words & Music by Reg Presley

# Love Shine A Light

Words & Music by Kimberley Rew

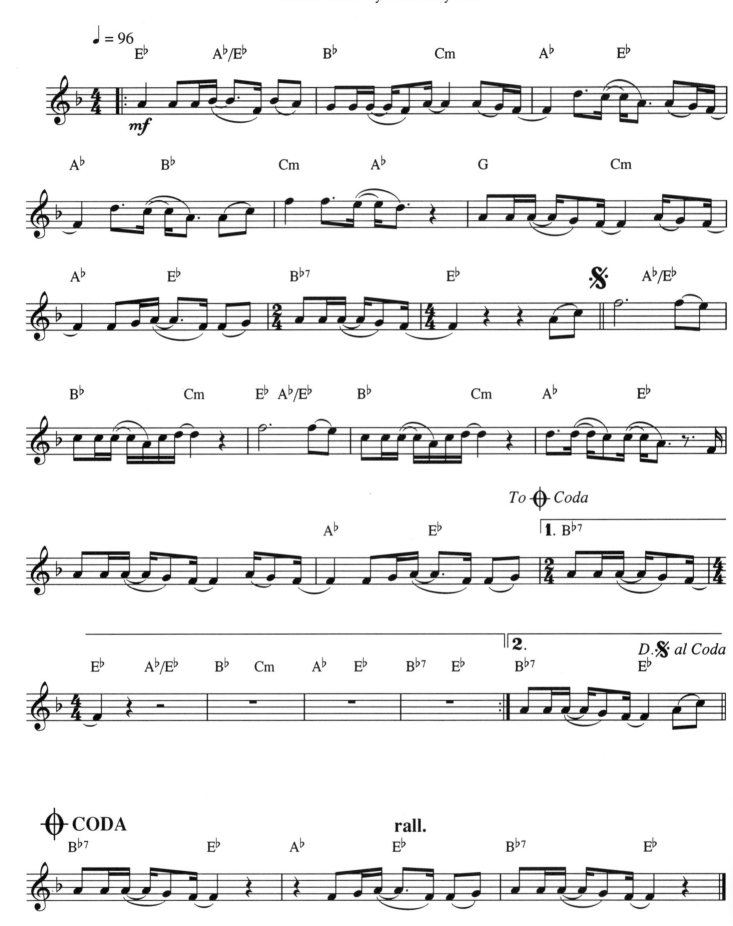

# Maria

Words & Music by Jimmy Destri

# Marvellous

Words & Music by Ian Broudie

# Message In A Bottle

Words & Music by Sting

# Mi Chico Latino

Words & Music by Geri Halliwell, Andy Watkins & Paul Wilson

# Missing

Words & Music by Tracey Thorn & Ben Watt

# Mrs Robinson

Words & Music by Paul Simon

# My All

Words by Mariah Carey
Music by Mariah Carey & Walter Afanasieff

# Nights In White Satin

Words & Music by Justin Hayward

# Night Fever

*Words & Music by Barry Gibb, Robin Gibb & Maurice Gibb*

# Oliver's Army

Words & Music by Elvis Costello

# Penny Lane

Words & Music by John Lennon & Paul McCartney

# Picture Of You

Words & Music by Eliot Kennedy, Ronan Keating, Paul Wilson & Andy Watkins

# Rio

Words & Music by Duran Duran

# Rotterdam

Words & Music by Paul Heaton & David Rotheray

# Runaway

Words & Music by Andrea Corr, Caroline Corr, Sharon Corr & Jim Corr

# Say You'll Be There

Words & Music by Eliot Kennedy, Jon B, Victoria Aadams,
Melanie Brown, Emma Bunton, Melanie Chisholm & Geri Halliwell

# Search For The Hero

### Words & Music by Mike Pickering & Paul Heard

# She's The One

Words & Music by Karl Wallinger

# So Young

Words & Music by Andrea Corr, Caroline Corr, Sharon Corr & Jim Corr

# Some Might Say

Words & Music by Noel Gallagher

# Something

Words & Music by George Harrison

# Space Oddity

Words & Music by David Bowie

# Stop

Words & Music by Victoria Aadams, Emma Bunton, Melanie Brown,
Melanie Chisholm, Geri Halliwell, Andy Watkins & Paul Wilson

# Stay Another Day

Words & Music by Tony Mortimer, Robert Kean & Dominic Hawken

# Take A Chance On Me

Words & Music by Benny Andersson & Björn Ulvaeus

# Take My Breath Away

Words by Tom Whitlock
Music by Giorgio Moroder

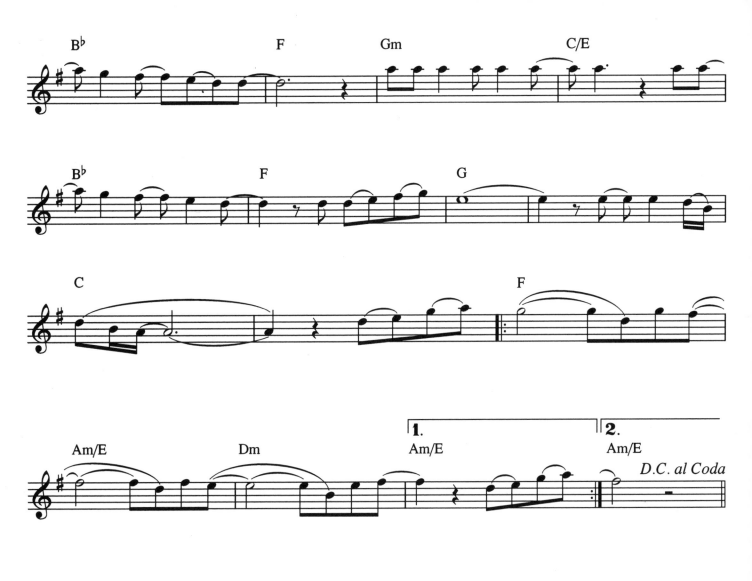

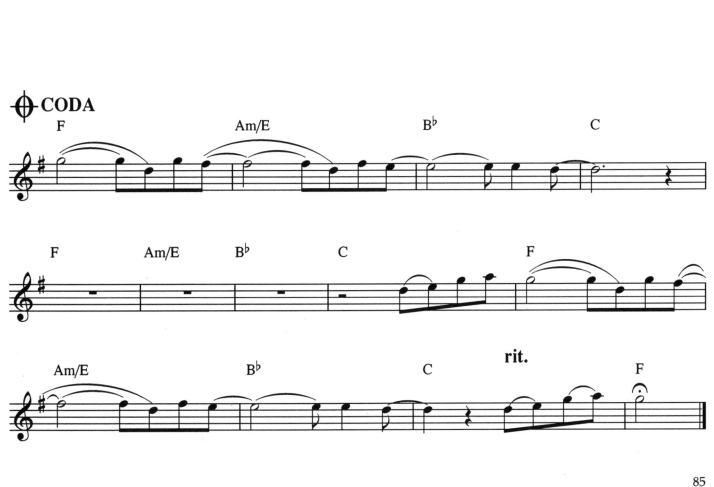

# Thank U

Words by Alanis Morissette
Music by Alanis Morissette & Glen Ballard

# That's The Way (I Like It)

### Words & Music by Harry Casey & Richard Finch

# Three Lions

**Words by David Baddiel & Frank Skinner**
**Music by Ian Broudie**

# Three Little Birds

Words & Music by Bob Marley

# To The End

Words & Music by Damon Albarn, Graham Coxon, Alex James & David Rowntree

# Torn

Words & Music by Anne Preven, Scott Cutler & Phil Thornalley

91

# Tragedy

Words & Music by Barry Gibb, Robin Gibb & Maurice Gibb

# Turn

### Words & Music by Fran Healy

# Turn Back Time

Words & Music by Søren Rasted, Claus Norreen, Johnny Pederson & Karsten Delgado

# 2 Become 1

Words & Music by Victoria Aadams, Melanie Brown, Emma Bunton,
Melanie Chisholm, Geri Halliwell, Matt Rowe & Richard Stannard

# Voulez-Vous

**Words & Music by Benny Andersson & Björn Ulvaeus**

# Waterloo Sunset

Words & Music by Ray Davies

# What Can I Do

Words & Music by Andrea Corr, Caroline Corr, Sharon Corr & Jim Corr

# When I Need You

Words & Music by Albert Hammond & Carole Bayer Sager

# When The Going Gets Tough

Words & Music by Wayne Braithwaite, Barry Eastmond, Robert John 'Mutt' Lange & Billy Ocean

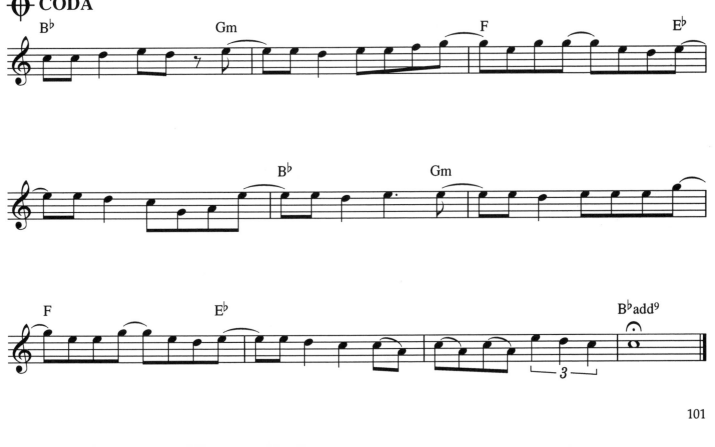

# When You Say Nothing At All

Words & Music by Paul Overstreet & Don Schlitz

# When You're Gone

Words & Music by Bryan Adams & Eliot Kennedy

# Who's That Girl?

Words & Music by Annie Lennox & David A. Stewart

# Words

Words & Music by Barry Gibb, Robin Gibb & Maurice Gibb

# Wonderful Tonight

Words & Music by Eric Clapton

# You Do Something To Me

Words & Music by Paul Weller

# You Gotta Be

Words & Melody by Des'ree
Music by Ashley Ingram

109

# You Must Love Me

Words by Tim Rice
Music by Andrew Lloyd Webber

# You're Still The One

Words & Music by Shania Twain & R.J. Lange

# Young At Heart

Words & Music by Robert Hodgens, Siobhan Fahey, Keren Woodward & Sarah Dallin